Phonics

Hi, everyone! It's your pal CJ here! Edison and I are about to blast off for outer space in our super-cool rocket. We'll visit new worlds, and we'll see strange new creatures. We'll also explore sounds, letters, and all kinds of phonics fun! You can help guide us through space and get us out of space jams. Zip up your space suits, here we go!

See these passport stamps? Every time you finish learning something new, you get one of these stickers to put on your passport. When you finish each section, you'll get a big adventurer's sticker to put on your Certificate of Completion!

Take a look at this picture of me. When you see this in the book, it means I'm there to give you a little help. Just look for **CJ's Clues**.

 ## CJ's Clues

Blends are two consonants put together. If you listen to a blend, you can hear each letter, like this: **s-p-ace, space**.

It's time to take off for the planets and stars! Let's get packing! Can you help us find things to take with us?

Say each picture name and circle the words that start with a blend.

flag

clock

grapes

book

saw

dragon

lemonade

skate

We're ready to blast off into space! We just need plenty of fuel for our spaceship. Help us fill up.

Read the word under each fuel can. Draw a line from the spaceship to the fuel cans whose picture words begin with blends.

flower

girl

snail

fish

grapes

star

glove

paintbrush

Can you add pictures that start with the blends beneath these cans?

cl

st

Great job! Put your stamp sticker on your passport and jump ahead to the next level!

Blends 3

Level 1

Let's see what s-blends are in the sky!
Connect the dots in each group of stars to make a picture, then say each name. What two beginning sounds do you hear? Write the first two sounds for each word.

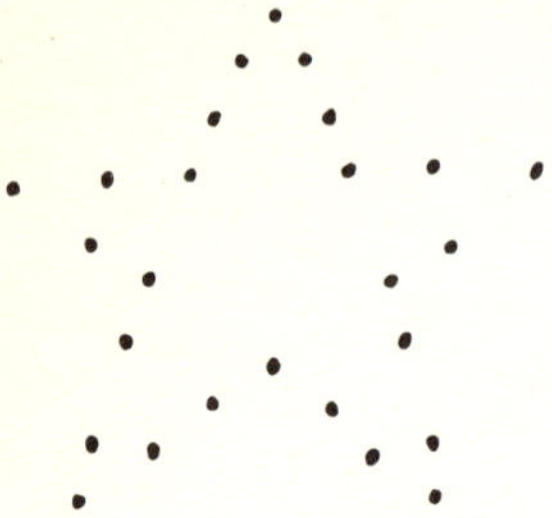

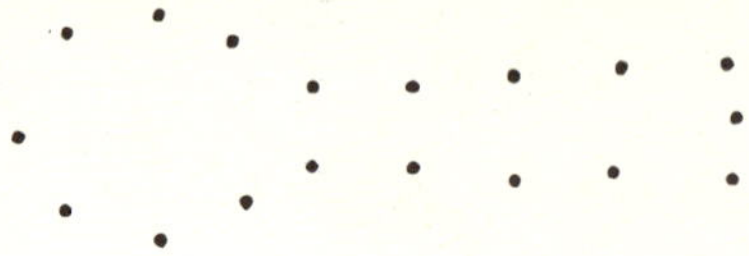

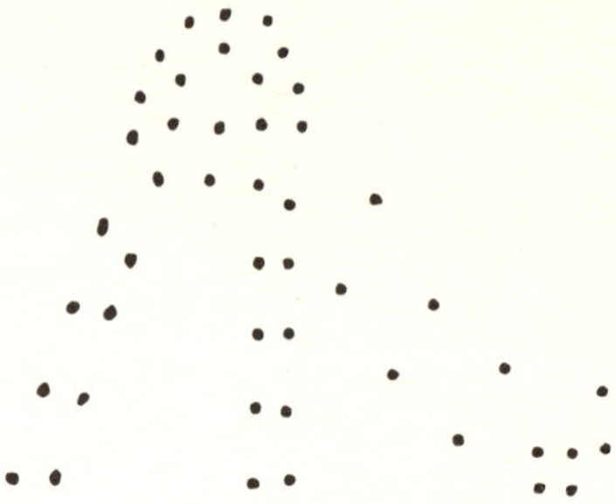

__oon

__ar

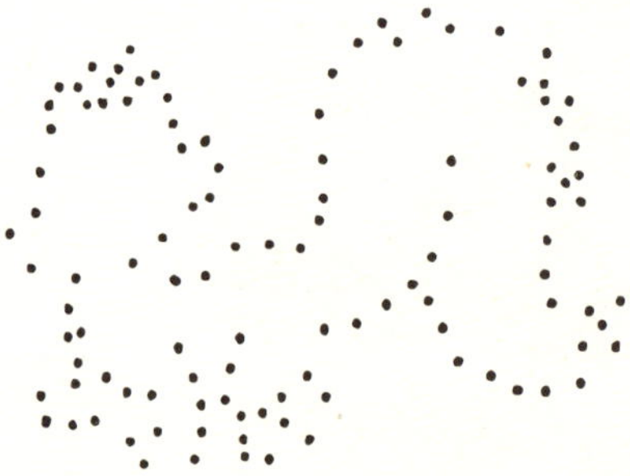

__ide

__unk

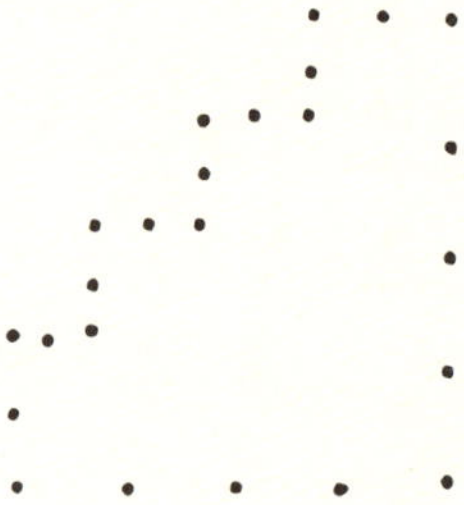

__eps

__ake

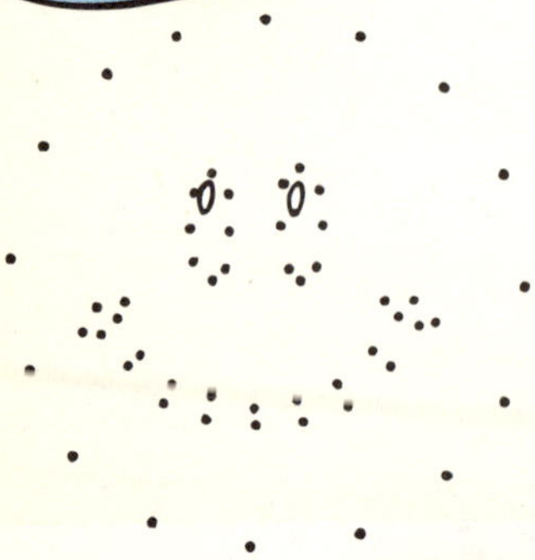

What word that starts with an s-blend would you use here? Write the beginning blend for your answer on the line. Then try to spell the whole word.

_____

4 Blends •

We're off!

These buttons have picture names that begin with l-blends. Write the blends on the correct lines.

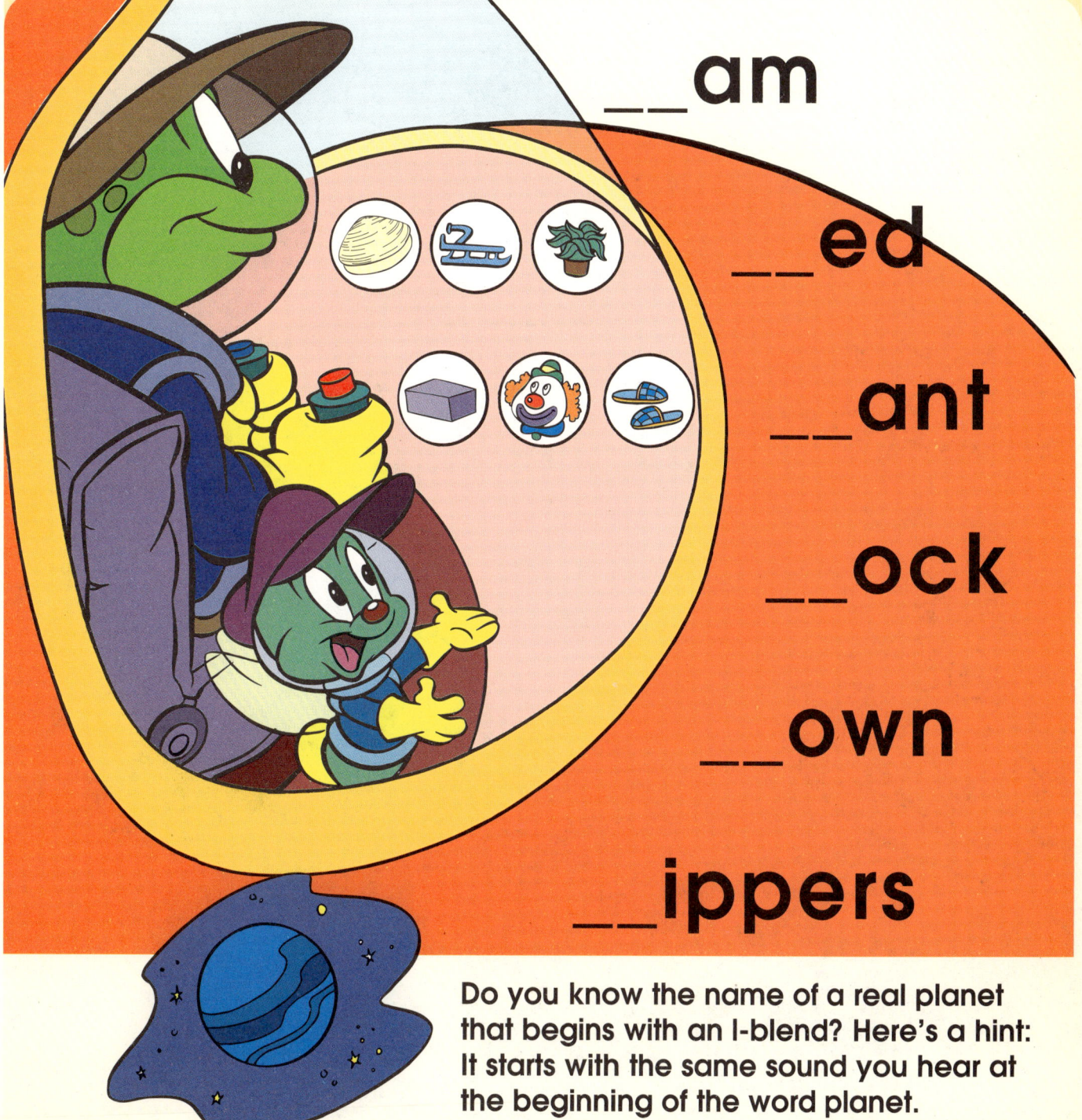

__am

__ed

__ant

__ock

__own

__ippers

Do you know the name of a real planet that begins with an l-blend? Here's a hint: It starts with the same sound you hear at the beginning of the word planet.

Oh, no! The creatures from planet Creepy are on their way to Earth! We have to stop them! Help us rocket past these asteroids. The only way out is to fill in r-blends.
Write the missing blends on the lines.

__og

__oom

__uck

__um

__ess   __ee

The Creepies made a pit stop on planet Plink! What did they bring with them?

Write the words that begin with s-blends, l-blends, or r-blends in the correct column.

s-blends | l-blends | r-blends

_____ | _____ | _____

_____ | _____ | _____

_____ | _____ | _____

_____ | _____ | _____

 clam

 bread

 snacks

 plane

 scooter

 blanket

 smock

 train

 grapes

 flashlight

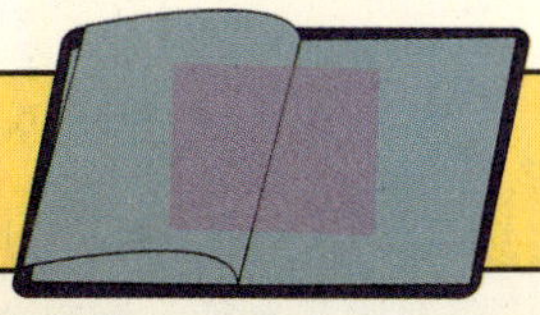

You're out of this world! Put your stamp sticker on your passport and jump ahead!

Blends 7

We want to plant our flag on planet Plink. So do the Creepies. Help us get our flag in first.

Finish the word math in each flag to make a new word that starts with a three-letter blend like thrill!

thr + oat = _____

spl + ash = _____

sing - s + str = _____

thing - th + spr = _____

main - m + spr = _____

team - t + str = _____

Guess the name of the Creepies' leader. Change the beginning sounds of dreamer to the beginning sounds of scrub. Write the new word here:

_____

Let's leave Plink and head for home. Help us set the dials on our spaceship.

Name each picture and listen for the first three sounds. Find and circle those letters in the dial. Then write them on the lines.

Level 3

_ _ _ ing

_ _ _ eet

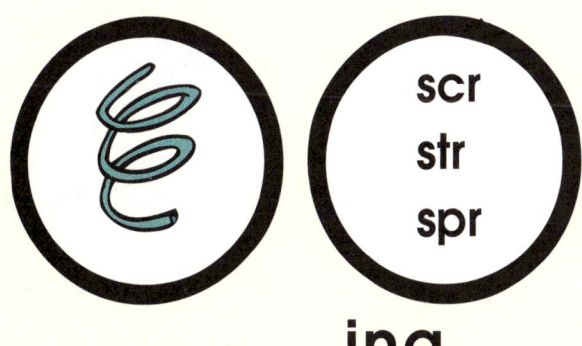

_ _ _ ing

_ _ _ one

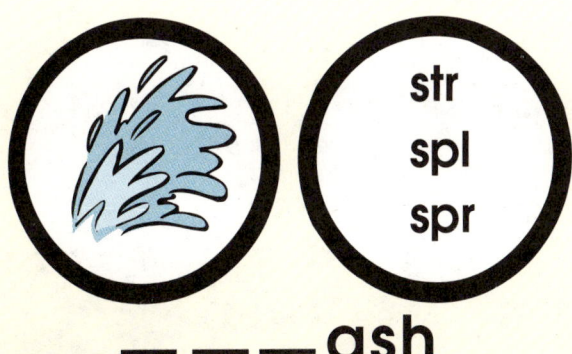

_ _ _ ash

Splendid! Put your stamp sticker on your passport and jump ahead!

Blends 9

Oh, no! The comet is headed our way! Help us move fast!

Circle the five words in each puzzle that begin or end in blends. The words can read down, across, or diagonally.

```
h  e  l  p  k
m  b  l  s  w
c  a  e  r  f
n  d  n  e  b
g  l  a  s  s
s  p  o  t  c
```

```
w  e  p  p  s
s  a  t  c  p
n  w  r  b  r
a  e  a  o  a
p  s  i  l  i
t  i  n  t  n
```

_____   _____

Now let's send our friends on Earth a message.

Look for the hidden word in the first line across in each letter box. Write it on the lines below to read what we said.

a	r	e	m	s
c	c	r	a	b
o	l	b	s	d
s	a	p	k	l
c	p	r	n	t
d	r	a	i	n

l	o	s	t	g
b	n	c	h	r
s	t	a	r	i
m	d	r	o	n
t	s	e	n	b
c	p	m	e	y

_____ _____

You did it! Put your constellation map sticker on the Certificate of Completion and jump ahead.

CJ's Clues

Digraphs are two consonants put together. If you listen to a digraph, you only hear one sound, like this: **sh-ip, ship**.

Look at that strange planet with six moons! Let's find out what's on each one.

Complete each word with a digraph.

| sh | ch | th | wh |

__ale

__air

__umb

fi __

__ell

__eese

Digraphs, Diphthongs, Silent Letters, Schwa

Brrrr! This place is chilly! Our rocket boosters are frozen. We will have to fix them, but our toolbox is so messy. Help us sort it out.

Draw a line between the toolbox spaces and the pictures with names that have the same sound at the beginning or end.

Level 1

| sh | th |
| ch | wh |

Circle the tool that would be the most useful tool for fixing a rocket. Can you spell its name?

_____

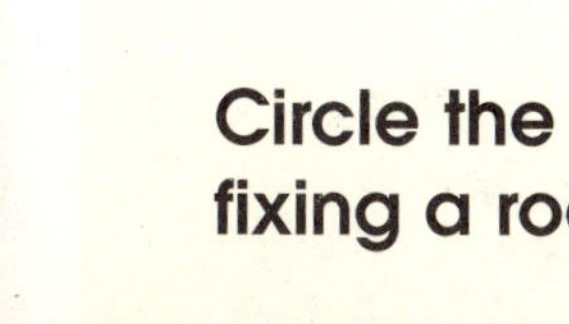

Great job! Put your stamp sticker on your passport and jump ahead!

Digraphs, Diphthongs, Silent Letters, Schwa

13

CJ's Clues

Diphthongs are two vowels that work together to make a new sound. B**oy** and c**oi**n are good examples. Sometimes the letter **y** acts as a vowel.

Way to go! We made it to the planet Doink. The Doinks only understand words with the "oi" sound! Help us decide what peace gift to give them. **Color all the words with Oi or Oy.** What do you see?

- chin
- hat
- oil
- soil
- toy
- plant
- hat
- boy
- drum
- noise
- bear
- shell
- dress
- choice
- foil
- point
- dress
- plate
- soft

What is in our gift box? It's a t _____ !

Digraphs, Diphthongs, Silent Letters, Schwa

The Doinks want us to help them find their lost cousins, the Zows. Follow the trail of picture words looking for those with the same vowel sound as Zow. **Put an X on the pictures with the OW sound.**

Level 2

You can spell the "ow" sound by using **OU**, as in blouse. Can you think of two words that are spelled with ou that will answer these riddles?

I am a small animal that runs from a cat. _____

I have a roof and four walls. You live in me. _____

Digraphs, Diphthongs, Silent Letters, Schwa

We've found the Zows. We wrote them a poem as a greeting, but we forgot to put in a few words. Will you help us?

Choose from the words below to finish the poem. All these words have the "ow" vowel sound spelled with OU.

around	shout
about	found
out	ground
out	sound

When our rocket hit the _____,

it made a _____.

We started to _____,

"Come _____, come _____!"

You were nowhere _____.

We walked all _____,

and guess what we _____?

You!

Oh, no! The Doinks did not like our poem because we didn't use any -oink words! We'd better get out of here. Help us find our way through the forest.

Read the words in the forest. Write them in the correct column.

Words that have the sound **"ow,"** like cow.

_____

_____

_____

_____

Words that have the vowel sound **"oy,"** like boy.

_____

_____

_____

_____

Great job! Put your stamp sticker on your passport and jump ahead!

Digraphs, Diphthongs, Silent Letters, Schwa

CJ's Clues

Sometimes when two consonants are together, the first one is silent. You don't hear the **"k"** sound in **kn**ee, do you?

We made it to our ship! Now we have to start it up very quietly, so the Doinks don't hear us.

Look at the rocket buttons below. Read the words in each button out loud. Circle each button that has a word with a silent consonant.

knee wrist not knife write

wrong wrench wreath need round

white knit right nine rent

18 Digraphs, Diphthongs, Silent Letters, Schwa

CJ's Clues

The first and last sound in b**a**nan**a** is a special vowel sound called **schwa**.

Hooray! We're zooming through space again. We need to read the stars to find our way.

Say each word out loud. Do you hear the sound of "a" as in about? If so, circle the word.

- after / amount
- answer / another 
- atom / away
- attic / awake
- athlete / ahead
- ant / agree 
- ape / above
- apple / alike

You did it! Put your stamp sticker on your passport and jump ahead!

Digraphs, Diphthongs, Silent Letters, Schwa

Level 3

It's a long trip home. Let's play a game while we're hurtling through space. Can you help us?

Read each clue below. Find the answer in the word box and write it in the correct space.

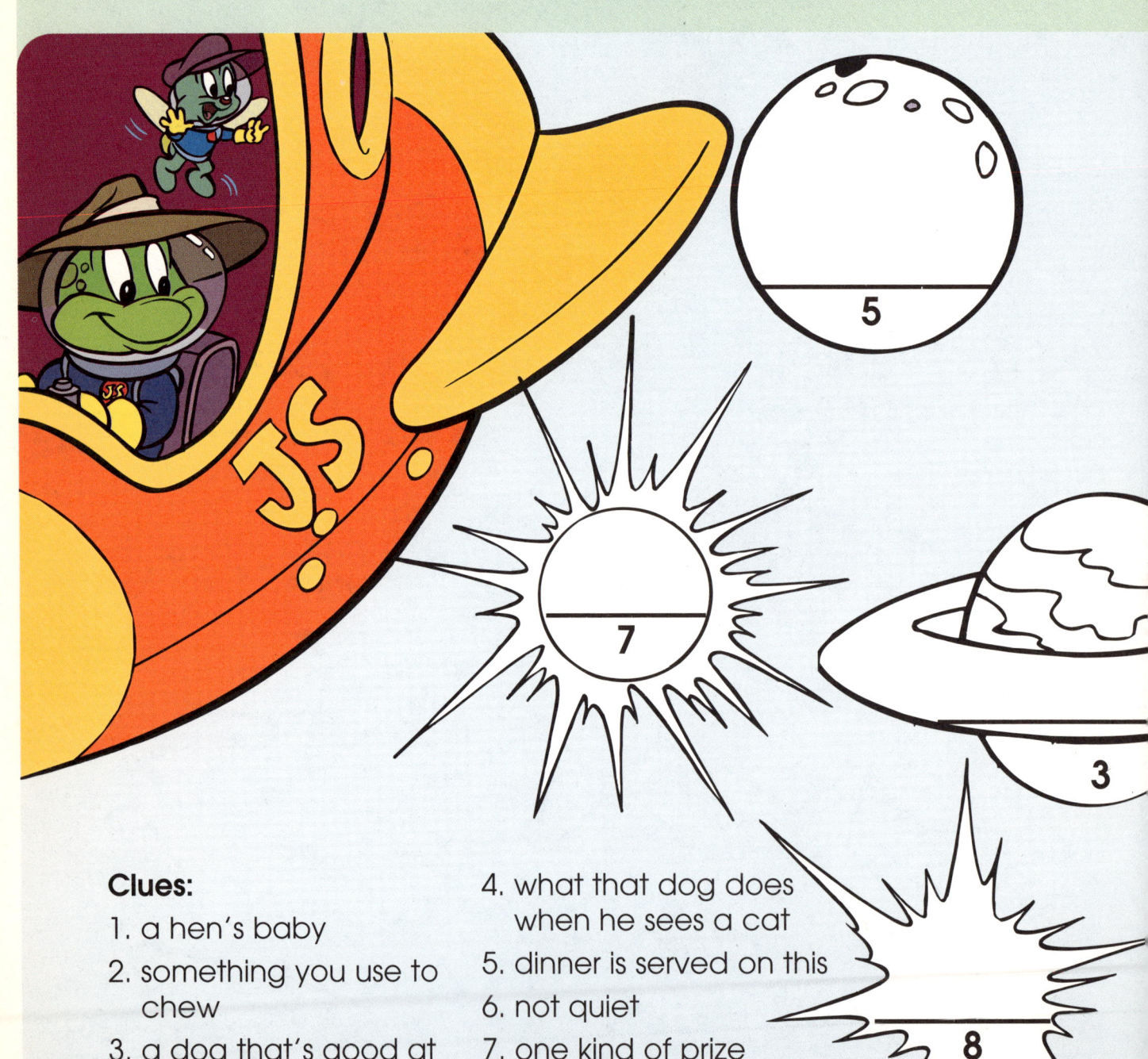

Clues:
1. a hen's baby
2. something you use to chew
3. a dog that's good at sniffing around
4. what that dog does when he sees a cat
5. dinner is served on this
6. not quiet
7. one kind of prize
8. the same as

loud　growls
dish　hound
teeth　award
alike　chick

You did it! Place your compass sticker on the Certificate of Completion and jump ahead!

Review

CJ's Clues

When you add the letter **r** to a vowel, it can change the vowel sound. The word **shack** has a short-a sound. But the word **shark** has a very different sound. So remember to watch for r's!

Oh, no! Our fuel meter is very low. We'll have to stop on Plink again. The Creepies are still here. They need us to help them build another spaceship.

Read each word in the spaceship on the left. Add the letter r after its vowel. Write your new word on the right.

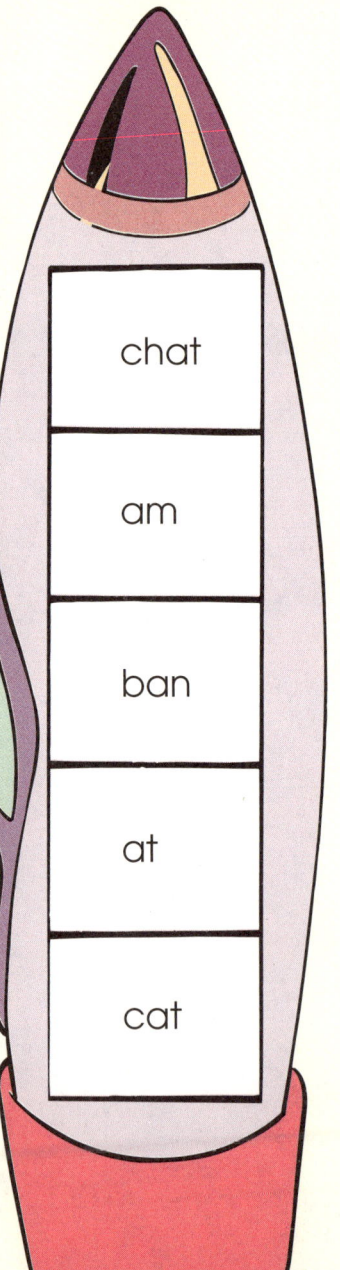

chat

am

ban

at

cat

The Creepies need help launching their new spaceship. Maybe it's because they can't tell a word like ch**ar**t from a word like ch**air**. Let's help them hear the different vowel sounds.

Answer the questions below by putting a check under the correct picture.

	chair	chart
car has the same vowel sound as	☐	☐
pear has the same vowel sound as	☐	☐
star has the same vowel sound as	☐	☐
bear has the same vowel sound as	☐	☐
square has the same vowel sound as	☐	☐
hair has the same vowel sound as	☐	☐

Look at your list of checks under chair. How many different ways can you write this vowel sound?

_____   _____   _____

Splendid! Put your stamp sticker on your passport and jump ahead to the next level.

Variant Vowels

The Creepies want to use their new spaceship to invade Earth. We've got to stop them! **Color all the Creepies' spaceship parts that have words with the vowel sound you hear in burn.**

We're hurtling through space again. Let's visit the planet Mupiter. Do you hear the sound that **"er"** makes in this word? Let's find things with that same sound on this planet.

Write er on the lines.

fath____

p____son

moth____

bak____

farm____

cam____a

lett____

show____

Write the letters s, u, and p on the lines to make a word that means great. Write your new word because this is what you are!

____ ____ ____ +er= _____

Edison wants to stop on planet Twirl. He wants to see what is on each of the planet's rings.

Can you help him find words with the same vowel sound as twirl? Write them on each ring. Choose from these words:

girl   skirt   circus   bird   shirt   thirteen   squirt   dirt

Look at the colors of these rings. They look like our favorite ice cream! What could it be? Write the letters **ir** on the line to find out.

rainbow sw ____ l

We're on planet Murk! It's so dark here, I can't see anything. Can you help me find my way back to Edison?

Fill in the stars with one of the words that have the sound ur as in Murk.

fur curb hurry purse turn curly

She ran fast. She was in a _____.

My cat has black _____.

She put a bow in her _____ hair.

Stop at the _____.
Look both ways before crossing.

The coins were in my mother's _____.

He had to _____ the knob to open the door.

On a separate piece of paper, draw something that might be lurking on planet Murk.

Magnificent! Put your stamp sticker on your passport and jump ahead!

CJ's Clues

When you put two **O**'s together, you can get different sounds. Say these words out loud.

moon    book

Edison is reading a book about space. He wants to visit more places, but I'm hungry. Help us decide what to do.

Write all the words that sound like book on Edison's side. Write all the words that sound like food on my side.

look	drool	fool	good
hook	poodle	noodle	shook
spool	took	tool	hood

food

book

Can you solve this riddle?
After you eat food, you can sweep up the crumbs with me.

I am a _____.

We're home! Many different kinds of rockets have come to meet us. They all have words with vowels that sound the same, but are spelled differently.

Look at the word on the tip of each rocket. Then circle the words in the rocket stream that have the same vowel sound as the word on the tip.

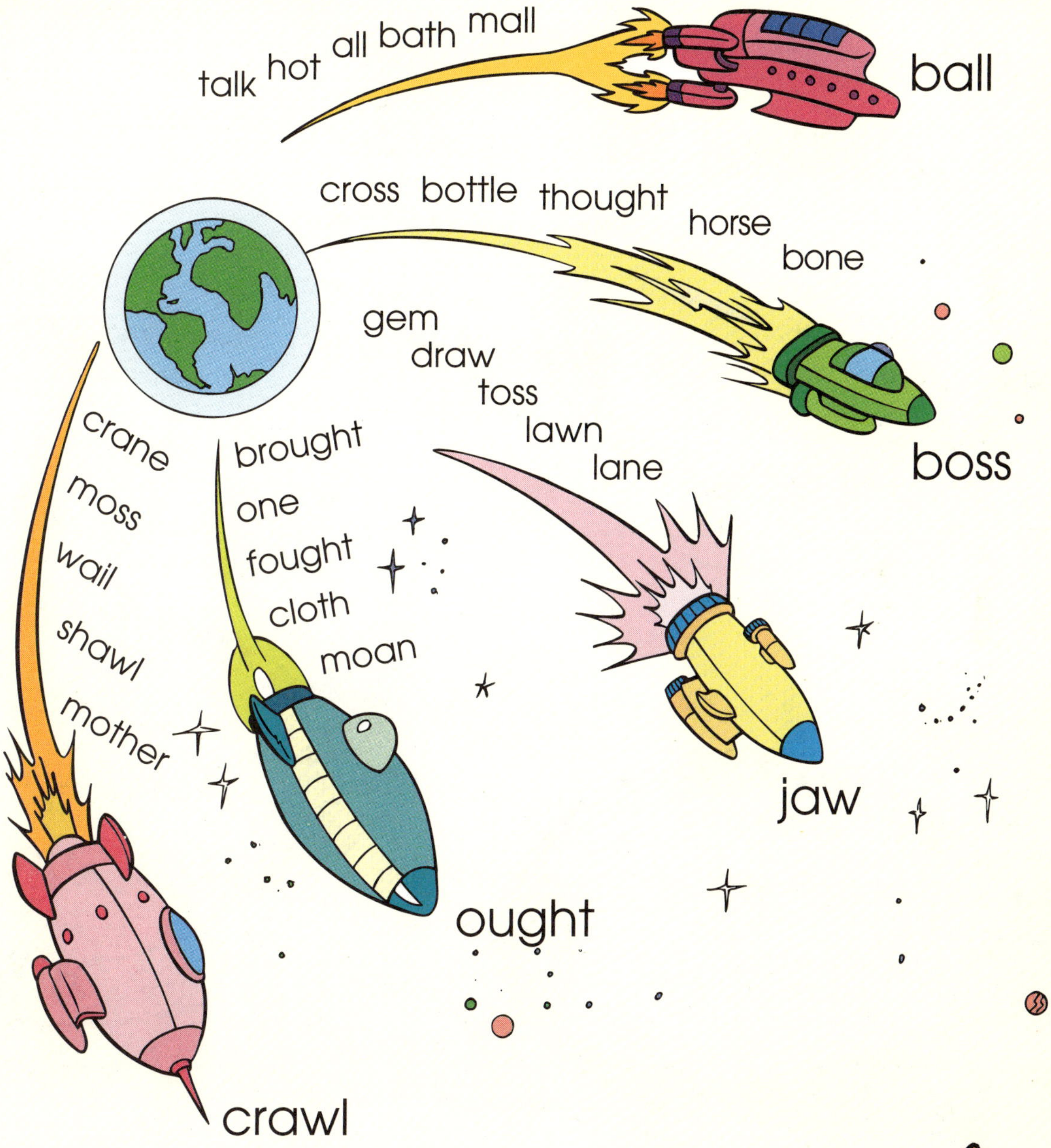

talk hot all bath mall   **ball**

cross bottle thought horse bone   **boss**

gem draw toss lawn lane   **jaw**

crane moss wail shawl mother   **crawl**

brought one fought cloth moan   **ought**

Can you write a word with the same vowel sound you found in all the words above? Hint: It's another way to say good-bye.

We're going home! So ____ ____ ____ ____ !

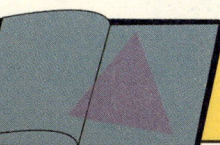

Great job! Put your stamp sticker on your passport and jump ahead!

Variant Vowels

We are heroes! Look at those blimps. Can you read what they say about us?
Use ar, er, ir, ur, all, or au to finish the words.

You l_____nched your rocket into deep, d_____k space.

Welcome back!

You wh_____led around space.

You are sup_____ and so sm_____t.

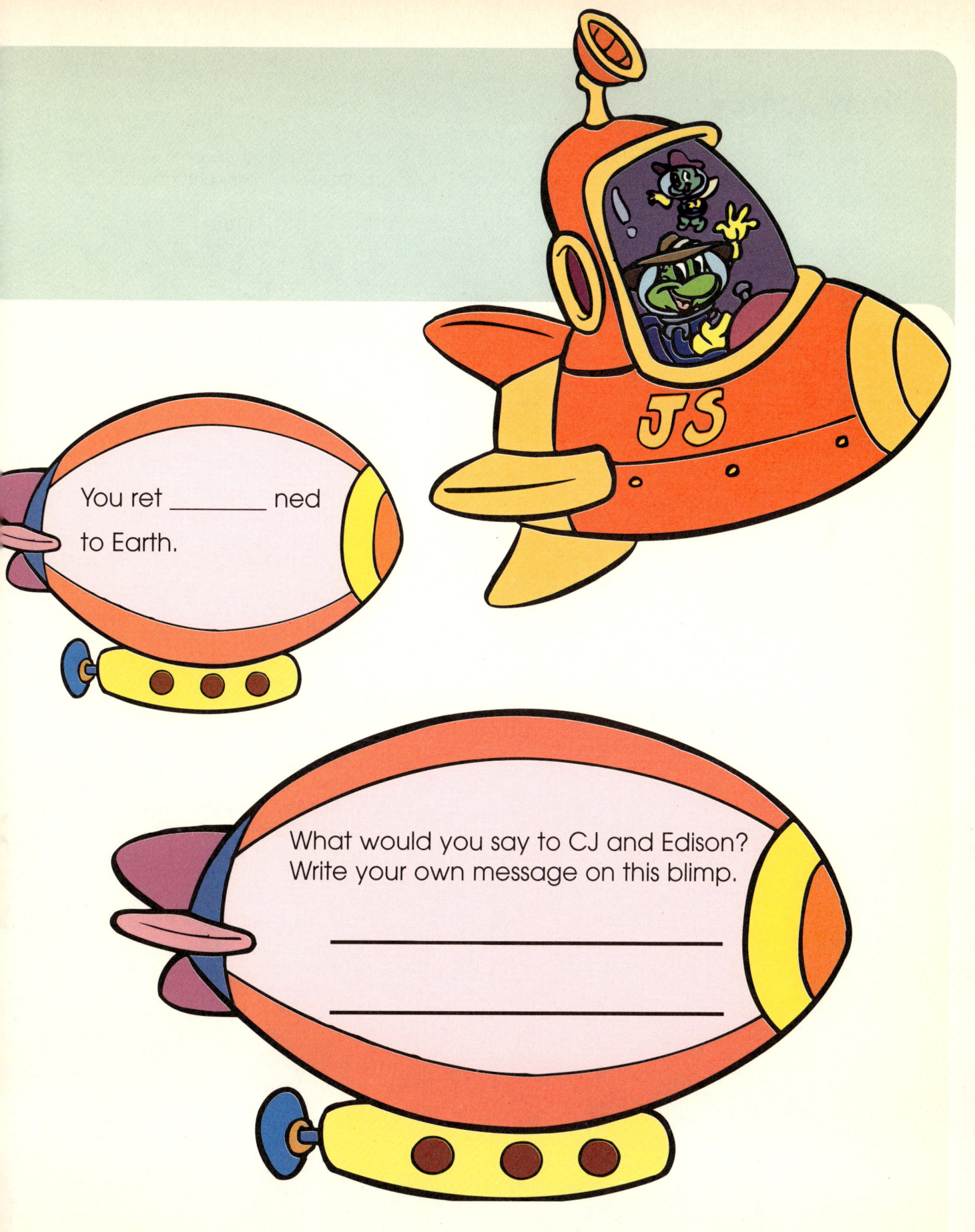

You ret _____ ned to Earth.

What would you say to CJ and Edison? Write your own message on this blimp.

_____

_____

Out of sight! You've earned your own space suit and helmet. Put that sticker on your Certificate of Completion.

Variant Vowels 31

Answer Key

PAGE 2	flag, clock, grapes, dragon, skate
PAGE 3	flower, snail, grapes, glove, star
PAGE 4	star, spoon, steps, slide, snake, skunk; smile
PAGE 5	clam, sled, plant, block, clown, slippers; Pluto
PAGE 6	broom, frog, truck, drum, tree, dress
PAGE 7	s-blends: snacks, scooter, smock, l-blends: clam, plane, blanket, flashlight r-blends: bread, train, grapes
PAGE 8	throat, splash, string, spring, sprain, stream; Screamer
PAGE 9	string, street, spring, throne, splash
PAGES 10–11	Puzzle 1: glass, spot, bend, rest, desk, plan, or help; Puzzle 2: snap, train, bolt, sprain, or tint; Puzzle 3: clap, crab, mask, or drain; Puzzle 4: scare, throne, grin, star, nest, or lost; Help we are lost
PAGE 12	whale, chair, thumb; fish, shell, cheese
PAGE 13	cherry, teeth, shark, dish, wheelbarrow, wrench, thermometer; wrench
PAGE 14	oil, toy, boy, noise, choice, foil, point; bear
PAGE 15	cross out cow, flower, shower, tower, clown; mouse
PAGE 16	ground, sound, shout, out, out, about, around, found
PAGE 17	pound, cloud, blouse, town; boil, toy, joy, noise
PAGE 18	knee, wrist, knife, write, wrong, wrench, wreath, white, knit, right
PAGE 19	above, ahead, awake, away, agree, alike, amount, another
PAGES 20–21	1. chick; 2. teeth; 3. hound; 4. growls; 5. dish; 6. loud; 7. award; 8. alike
PAGE 22	chart, arm, barn, art, cart
PAGE 23	chair: pear, bear, square, hair; chart: car, star; ear, are, air
PAGE 24	bird, stir, squirt, fur, fir, germ, fern, nerve, dirt
PAGE 25	father, person, baker, farmer, mother, camera, letter, shower; super
PAGE 26	skirt, circus, dirt, shirt, thirteen, squirt, bird, girl; swirl
PAGE 27	hurry, fur, curly, curb, purse, turn
PAGE 28	food: spool, drool, poodle, fool, noodle, tool; book: look, hook, took, good, hood, shook; broom
PAGE 29	rocket 1: talk, all, mall rocket 2: cross, thought rocket 3: draw, toss, lawn rocket 4: brought, fought, cloth rocket 5: shawl, moss; long
PAGES 30–31	blimp words: launched, dark, whirled, returned, super, smart

Reading & Writing

Hi, it's me, CJ! I am so excited! I found an old map that leads to a long-lost treasure! My buddy Edison and I are going to look for it. Come help us find the clues that will lead us to the treasure. Let's go!

See these passport stamp stickers? Every time you finish learning something new, you get one of these stickers to put in your passport. When you finish a whole section, you'll get a cool adventurer's sticker to put on your Certificate of Completion!

See this picture of me? When you see it in the book, it means I'm there to give you a little help. Just look for **CJ's Clues!**

CJ's Clues

Syllables are beats in a word. **Map** has one syllable, and **ca-mel** has two. Syllables in poetry give a poem its rhythm.

Our first stop is Egypt. Our first clue is this poem. Count the syllables in the underlined words. **Write the number of syllables on each line.**

The treasure you seek, _____

Is over that peak. _____

The pyramid, too, _____

Has a clue for you. _____

Adventure is fun. _____

Keep cool in the sun. _____

The desert is hot. _____

This looks like the spot! _____

Here's another clue to the lost treasure. It's written as a special rhyming poem called a **limerick.** A limerick syllable pattern is always the same.
Read this limerick out loud. Then write the number of syllables in each line of poetry below.

There once was a frog named CJ, _____

Who hunted for treasure all day. _____

He added up clues, _____

In one's and in two's, _____

And then went exploring that way! _____

Great job! Put your stamp sticker on your passport and jump ahead to the next level!

Poetry 35

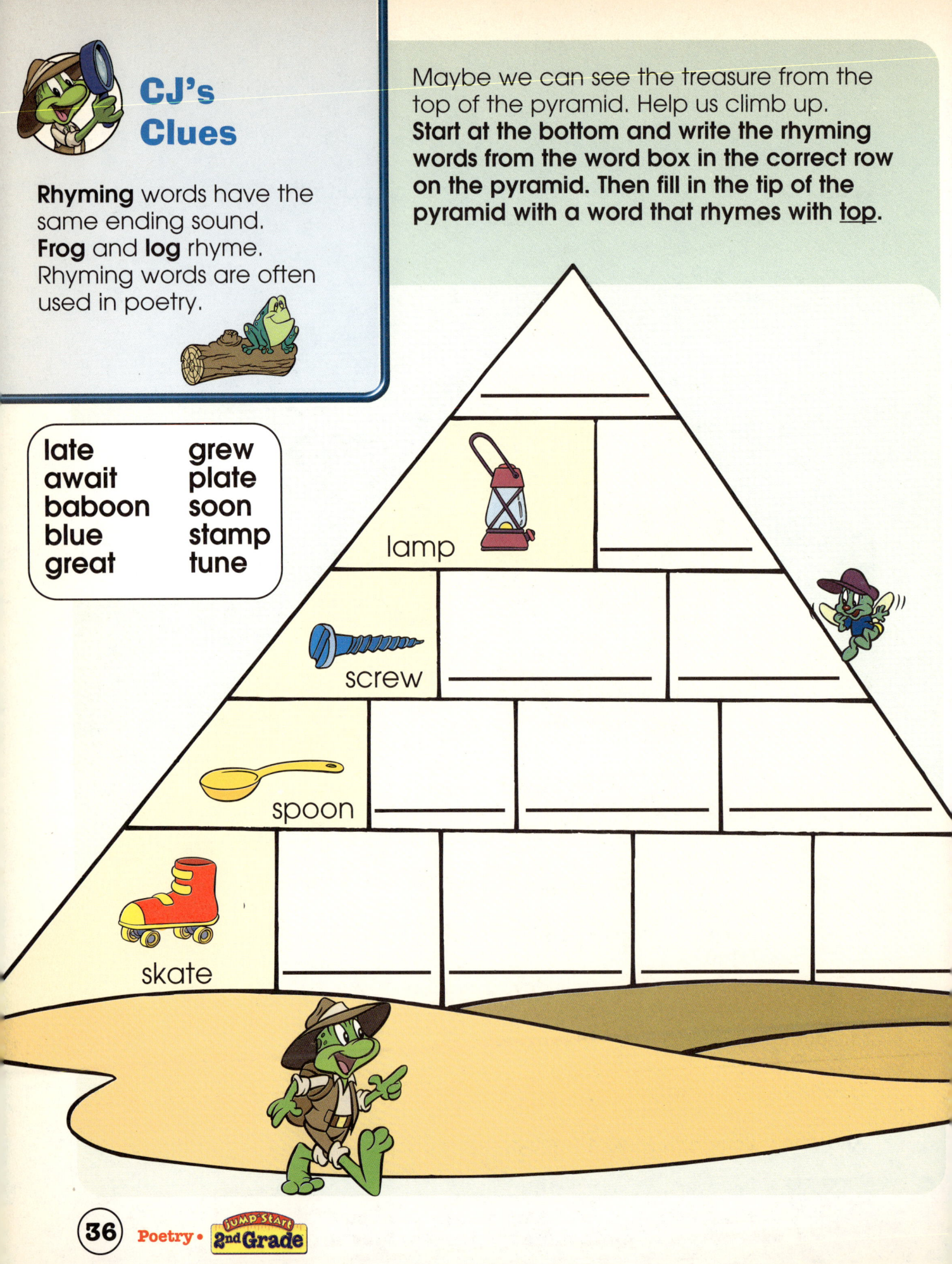

Help us solve the Sphinx's riddles so we can go inside. **Use the correct rhyming words from the scroll.**

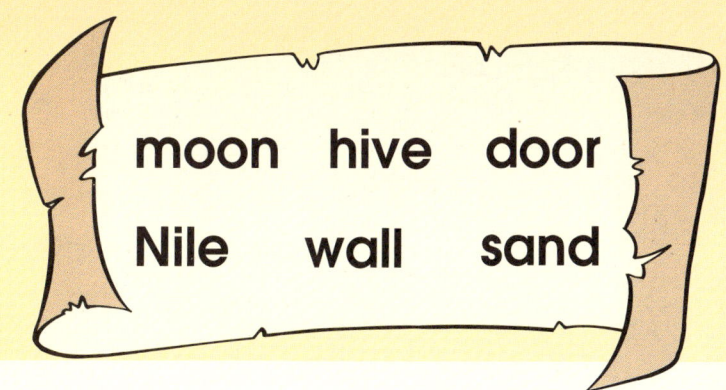

moon hive door
Nile   wall sand

I am the way into a room.
I rhyme with **chore.** What am I?

_____

I can hold up a home.
I rhyme with **fall.** What am I?

_____

I cover the desert.
I rhyme with **band.** What am I?

_____

I shine in the sky.
I rhyme with **noon.** What am I?

_____

I am a river in Egypt.
I rhyme with **pile.** What am I?

_____

I am a home for bees.
I rhyme with **dive.** What am I?

_____

Now it's our turn to ask the Sphinx a riddle. Do you know the answer? Write it on the line.

I am not hello.
I rhyme with **rye.** What am I?

_____

Poetry

This way could be booby-trapped! We should only step on rhyming-word pairs.

Draw X's on the rhyming words in each row of stones.

batter	big	when	coat
batch	bright	bleach	flute
champ	light	bench	boat
chatter	lit	wrench	soft
matter	fight	peach	goat

We made it! What do you think we will find inside?

_____

_____

_____

This mummy sure is chummy! He wants to share his gold coins.

Read the words on the chests. Then write three rhyming words next to each one that starts with the letters on each coin. Now we're in the money!

Level 2

 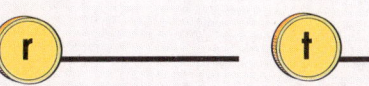 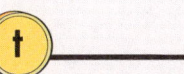

 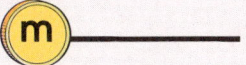 

Great job! Put your stamp sticker on your passport and jump ahead to the next level!

Poetry 39

Look! There is more to be found. **Use these rhyming words to finish the poem and get another clue.**

| nearer | jewels | chest |
| money | hold | |

That mummy sure was **funny**.
He gave you all his

___ ___ ___ ___ ___ .
　　　　　3

You won't need any **tools**
to pull out these shiny

___ ___ ___ ___ ___ ___ .
　　　　　　7

Now you have a bag of **gold**
That's really heavy to

___ ___ ___ ___ .
5　　　9 & 10

This note will make things **clearer:**
You are getting

___ ___ ___ ___ ___ ___ .
　　　　　8　　　　　2

If you need help on your **quest,**
look deep inside this

___ ___ ___ ___ ___ .
　　　6　　　1 & 4

Now write the numbered letters on the numbered lines below for another clue.

___ ___ ___ ___ ___ ___
1　2　3　　4　5　6

___ ___ ___ ___ !
7　8　9　10

We're still looking for the big secret treasure. Let's stop to figure out this puzzling wall first!

Circle the words in each puzzle that rhyme with the word at the top. Go across, up and down, diagonally and backward. Then use one puzzle word to finish each sentence.

5 words rhyming with **might**

```
b  i  t  e  e  s
t  r  u  t  i  e
r  k  i  t  e  a
e  r  e  g  m  m
w  u  t  d  h  a
m  n  i  g  h  t
```

I **might** _____ you a letter tonight.

6 words rhyming with **chore**

```
s  n  o  r  e  d
r  o  f  d  n  r
u  o  r  y  o  a
o  a  l  y  e  o  p  w
f  l  o  o  r  e
k  s  r  i  g  r
```

Today my **chore** is to sweep the _____.

4 words rhyming with **eel**

```
s  p  i  b  l  p
h  q  u  h  e  m
r  o  u  e  r  l
v  f  f  e  e  l
m  e  a  l  a  l
l  x  l  u  b  l
```

If you saw an **eel**, would you _____?

5 words rhyming with **train**

```
s  p  a  i  n  z
m  l  l  u  l  t
r  a  e  a  x  r
a  i  n  b  n  a
i  n  r  e  w  e
n  e  n  a  m  n
```

You can ride in a **train**, but a _____ is faster.

Magnificent! Put your stamp sticker on your passport and jump ahead.

We're off!
Use the words from the cloud key to finish the poem. Then you'll know where we are going.

Peru pair site anywhere lead croak

On the sea or in the air,
Edison and I are quite the
_____.

Adventure is the thing we need.
You'll always find us in the
_____.

We like a laugh, we like a joke.
And one of us can really
_____.

Now we need a little light. This should help us find our _____.

We fly here and we fly there. We're willing to go _____.

We're looking for another clue. That's why we're going to _____.

You did it! Place your treasure map sticker on the Certificate of Completion and jump ahead!

CJ's Clues

A **sentence** is a complete thought. The first word of a sentence starts with a capital letter. Sentences end with a punctuation mark, such as a period, exclamation point, or question mark:

. ! ?

Let's ask this llama about the treasure. Only complete sentences will help us. **Circle each complete sentence in the llama's answers.**

1
To hike many more miles

Are you ready to hike many more miles?

2
You must look for old ruins.

You and old ruins

3
The ruins are very, very high up!

Up high are

4
But will there

You will find a clue up there.

Read the complete sentences in order and find out what CJ and Edison should do next.

The monkeys are trying to tell us something about the lost treasure.

Write the correct punctuation after each sentence.
- **.** Use a period for a sentence that tells something.
- **?** Use a question mark for a sentence that asks something.
- **!** Use an exclamation point when a sentence says something very strongly!

Hello there

The treasure is not here

Are you looking for the lost treasure

Have you tried the secret room

The treasure is so beautiful

Good luck

We've found the secret room!
We just have to put the punctuation in the message. Add a period, a question mark, or an exclamation point. Then we can open the door.

What have you found

This is a secret door

It will give you a clue

What will the clue tell you

Open the door to find out

What do you think we'll find on the other side of the door? Write your answer in a complete sentence.

_____

_____

_____

Sentence Writing

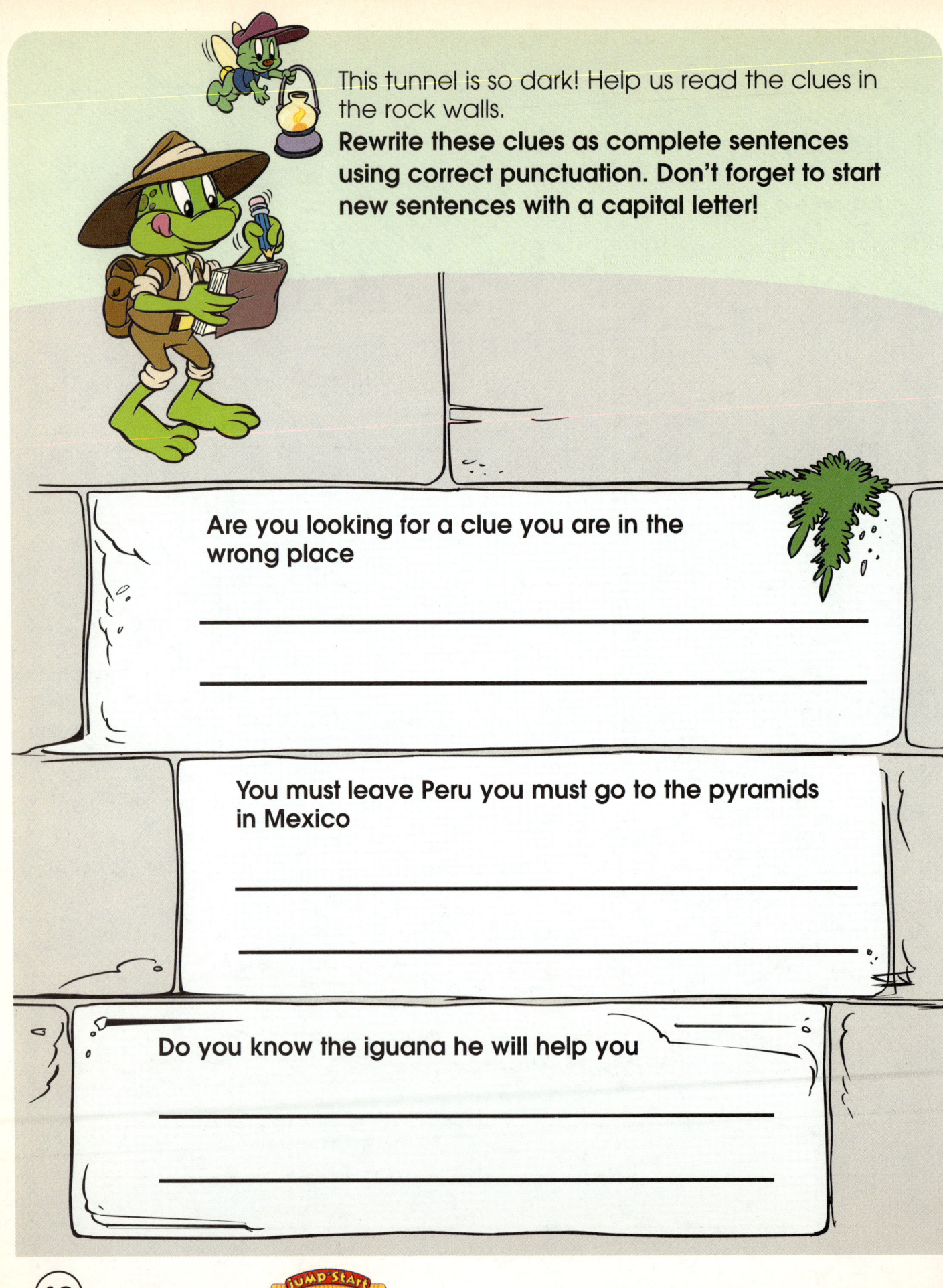

This tunnel is so dark! Help us read the clues in the rock walls.

Rewrite these clues as complete sentences using correct punctuation. Don't forget to start new sentences with a capital letter!

Are you looking for a clue you are in the wrong place

_____

_____

You must leave Peru you must go to the pyramids in Mexico

_____

_____

Do you know the iguana he will help you

_____

_____

We made it to Mexico! The iguana will help us. He is a friendly fellow, but he does run on!

Can you add punctuation marks in the correct places to separate his sentences?

Are you the fellows looking for the lost treasure   I do not know where it is   I think you can find a clue in the pyramid

Do you see the pyramid over there   Climb to the top   Good luck

Great job! Put your stamp sticker on your passport and jump ahead to the next level!

CJ's Clues

A **declarative** sentence is a statement. The noun comes before the verb.
The dog is tired.

In a **question** sentence, the verb comes before the noun.
Is the dog tired?

We will have to climb our way up.
Read the statements on the left. Look for the same thing turned into a question on the right. Fill in the missing word and then draw a line between the two.

The pyramid is very steep.   _____ the iguana helpful?

CJ is looking for a clue.   _____ Edison fly?

The iguana was helpful.   _____ CJ looking for a clue?

Edison can fly.   _____ the pyramid steep?

Look who we met inside! We can get the jewel if we change these questions into statements.
Will you help us? Write the questions as statements on the lines.

Do we want to find the lost treasure?

_____

_____

_____

Do we need to find a big river?

_____

_____

_____

Must we leave Mexico?

_____

_____

Should we go to the Grand Canyon?

_____

_____

Magnificent! Put your stamp sticker on your passport and jump ahead!

Sentence Writing

We have to cross the big river to continue.
Come with us! You just have to correct the sentences along the way. All sentences are missing punctuation. Some are missing words. Choose from the words in the box.

We are on our way

What are we looking for

Watch your step

_____ you thirsty ye

CJ's Clues

It is important to understand what you read. It helps to remember the **sequence of events**. This is the **order** in which things happen.

We have seen some amazing sights. **Can you remember what we saw first? And after that? And after that?** Look in my journal. Everything is all mixed up. Number the sentences in the order in which they happened. Look back if you need a reminder.

_____ We met a llama.

_____ The mummy gave us coins.

_____ We climbed up the Mexican pyramid.

_____ We met monkeys at the ruins.

_____ The iguana gave us a clue.

**Where do you think we will be going now?
Write your answer below using a complete sentence.**

_____

_____

The sentences in my journal are out of order. What do you think is the correct sequence?
First read each sentence. Then number the sentences in order to show what happened when.

_____ The snake told us a story.

_____ We got out of our canoe.

_____ We came to the end of the river.

_____ We met a snake.

Way to go! Put your stamp sticker on your passport and jump ahead!

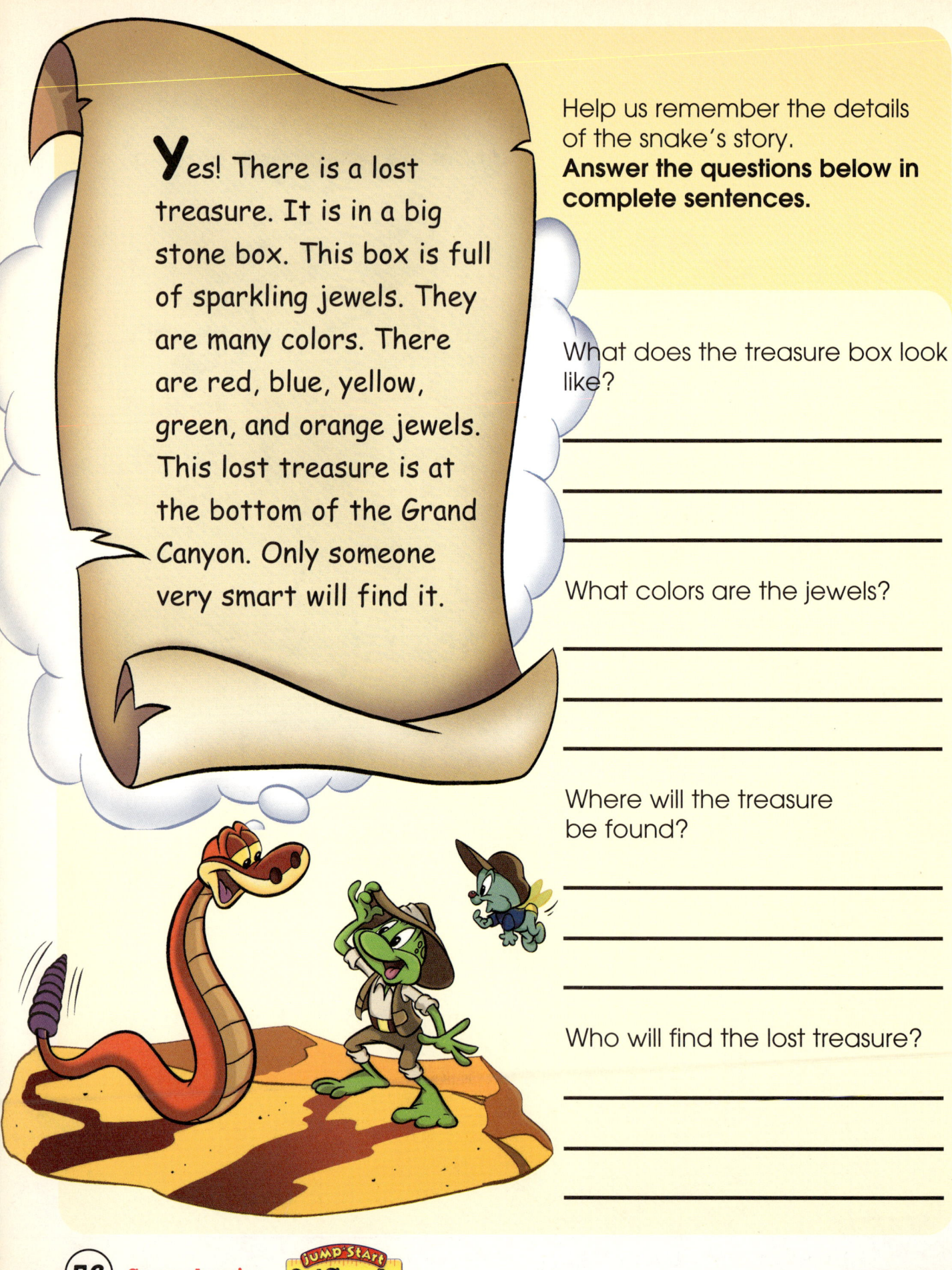

Yes! There is a lost treasure. It is in a big stone box. This box is full of sparkling jewels. They are many colors. There are red, blue, yellow, green, and orange jewels. This lost treasure is at the bottom of the Grand Canyon. Only someone very smart will find it.

Help us remember the details of the snake's story.
Answer the questions below in complete sentences.

What does the treasure box look like?
_____
_____
_____

What colors are the jewels?
_____
_____
_____

Where will the treasure be found?
_____
_____
_____

Who will find the lost treasure?
_____
_____
_____

The mule told us his story! Help us remember it all. **Answer the questions in complete sentences.**

I am a mule. I came to the canyon five years ago. I came with a man. He was looking for the lost treasure, too. This man did not like the canyon. It was too hot. There were snakes. The man did not like sleeping in a tent. He missed his home in the city. So the man left.

I liked the canyon. I liked the trails. I liked the beautiful sunsets. When the man left, I stayed. Now I help people get to the bottom of the canyon.

When did the mule come to the canyon?
_____
_____
_____
_____

Why did the man leave?
_____
_____
_____
_____

What was the man looking for?
_____
_____
_____
_____

What does the mule do now?
_____
_____
_____
_____

Look at this sign. Let's make sure we understand it.
Read the sign and circle the correct answers to the questions below.

Hello!

This message is for anyone looking for the lost treasure. It will be found by two smart treasure hunters. One is green. One can fly. Does this sound like you? If so, keep going!

1. Who is this message for?
   anyone
   no one
   the mule

2. Who will find the treasure?
   the mule
   treasure hunters
   the snake

3. What do they look like? Circle two.
   One is green.
   One is lost.
   One is old.
   One can swim.
   One can fly.
   One can sleep.

Here's an amazing legend a bird told us.
Let's make sure we understand it.
Answer the questions below in complete sentences.

The Legend of the Lost Treasure

Long ago, before there was day and night, there was only day. The Sun shone all the time. One day, the Moon rose in the sky. The Moon wanted a place in the sky, too. The Sun knew it would have to share. The Sun was sad. Now people would see its warm light only during the day. The Sun began to cry. Its tears turned into beautiful jewels. The jewels fell into the Grand Canyon. The animals there hid them in a safe place deep in the canyon. I can show you where they are.

Who shone first, the Sun or the Moon?

_____

_____

How did the Sun feel when the Moon came?

_____

_____

What happened to the Sun's tears?

_____

_____

Who hid the jewels?

_____

_____

Splendid! Put your stamp sticker on your passport and jump ahead to the next level!

CJ's Clues

An **opinion** is what you or someone else thinks about something.

Help us talk to the wolf! Read what he is saying to us and tell him why we are so smart.
Give your opinion in complete sentences.

I helped the other animals. We brought this heavy stone box down here. It is filled with treasure. We agreed to give it to whoever was smart enough to find it. Are you smart enough? Tell me why, and the treasure is all yours.

We are smart because _____

_____

_____

_____

_____

We've done it! We found the treasure.
Now tell us what you think in complete sentences.

Describe the treasure in your own words.

_____

_____

How could CJ and Edison get the treasure home?

_____

_____

Which piece of the treasure would you take home? Why?

_____

_____

Way to go! Put your stamp sticker on your passport and jump ahead!

Comprehension

This adventure is over. Now we can relax and read about our travels.
Read this newspaper story. Then fill in the crossword puzzle.

JumpStart Times

Lost Treasure Found!

Twenty other people tried to find the lost treasure but failed. Two fearless treasure hunters did it! CJ the Frog and Edison the Firefly made an awesome discovery. Yesterday they found the lost treasure in a stone box. The box was at the bottom of the Grand Canyon. It was full of jewels!

"We are thrilled to have found the treasure," said CJ. "We will share the treasure with the world."

"Yes," added Edison. "We will give the jewels to a museum."

CJ and Edison are our heroes!

Across:
1. Who will CJ and Edison give the lost treasure to?
4. What word describes CJ and Edison's discovery?
5. How many other people tried to find the treasure?
7. What are CJ and Edison called?

Down:
2. What kind of box was the treasure in?
3. Who will CJ and Edison share the treasure with?
6. How do CJ and Edison feel?

You've earned your own jewels! Put that sticker in your field book on your Certificate of Completion.

Answer Key

PAGE 34 2, 1, 3, 1, 3, 1, 2, 1

PAGE 35 8, 8, 5, 5, 8

PAGE 36 From bottom: await, great, late, plate; baboon, soon, tune; blue, grew; stamp; answers will vary.

PAGE 37 door, wall, sand, moon, Nile, hive; good-bye

PAGE 38 batter, chatter, matter; bright, light, fight; bench, wrench; coat, boat, goat; answers will vary.

PAGE 39 peach: reach, teach, bleach post: most, host, ghost sack: snack, tack, back

PAGE 40 money, hold, chest, jewels, nearer; Try the wall!

PAGE 41 bite, bright, kite, write, night; snore, sore, drawer, floor, four, or; squeal, meal, heel, feel; rain, pain, mane, plane, plain; write, floor, squeal, plane

PAGES 42–43 pair, lead, croak, site, anywhere, Peru

PAGE 44
1. Are you ready to hike many more miles?
2. You must look for old ruins.
3. The ruins are very, very high up!
4. You will find a clue up there.

PAGE 45 Complete sentences are: You have come a long way.
What do you seek?
These ruins are very old.
Monkeys live in this one.

PAGE 46 Hello there!
Are you looking for the lost treasure?
The treasure is so beautiful!
The treasure is not here.
Have you tried the secret room?
Good luck!

PAGE 47 What have you found?
This is a secret door.
It will give you a clue.
What will the clue tell you?
Open the door to find out!
Answers will vary.

PAGE 48 Are you looking for a clue?
You are in the wrong place.
You must leave Peru.
You must go to the pyramids in Mexico.
Do you know the iguana?
He will help you.

PAGE 49 Are you the fellows looking for the lost treasure?
I do not know where it is. I think you can find a clue in the pyramid. Do you see the pyramid over there? Climb to the top. Good luck!

PAGE 50 The pyramid is very steep./Is the pyramid steep?
CJ is looking for a clue./Is CJ looking for a clue?
The iguana was helpful./Was the iguana helpful?
Edison can fly./Can Edison fly?

PAGE 51 We want to find the lost treasure.
We must leave Mexico.
We need to find a big river.
We should go to the Grand Canyon.

PAGES 52–53 We are on our way.
What are we looking for?
Watch your step!
Are you thirsty yet?
What is that plant called? **It** is a cactus.
Ouch!
This is fun! I like the desert.
Will we find the treasure?
You bet **we will** find the treasure!
Are you hot? Yes, **I am** hot.
We made it across!

PAGE 54 2, 1, 5, 3, 4; answers will vary.

PAGE 55 4, 2, 1, 3

PAGE 56 Exact wording may vary, but main ideas are:
It is a big stone box.
The jewels are red, blue, yellow, green, and orange.
The treasure is at the bottom of the Grand Canyon.
Someone very smart will find it.

PAGE 57 Exact wording may vary, but the main ideas are:
The mule came to the canyon five years ago.
The man was looking for the lost treasure.
The man left because he did not like the canyon. The man did not like snakes. The man did not like to sleep in a tent. The man missed his home in the city.
The mule helps people get to the bottom of the canyon.

PAGE 58 1. anyone 2. treasure hunters 3. One is green./One can fly.

PAGE 59 Exact wording may vary, but the main ideas are:
The Sun shone first.
The Sun was sad.
The Sun's tears became jewels.
The animals hid the jewels.

PAGE 60 Answers will vary.

PAGE 61 Answers will vary.

PAGE 63

Crossword answers:
1. MUSEUM
3. WORLD
4. AWESOME
5. TWENTY
6. THRILLED
7. HEROES
(Down from MUSEUM: TON)

Math

Hi, it's me, CJ! I am so excited! We're going on an underwater adventure! Come along and see what happens in the wet, wet world underwater.

See these passport stamp stickers? Every time you finish learning something new, you get one of these stickers to put on your passport. When you finish a whole section, you'll get a cool adventurer's sticker to put on your Certificate of Completion!

See this picture of me? When you see it in the book, it means I'm there to give you a little help. Just look for **CJ's Clues**!

So, are you ready? Let's dive down, down, down.

Introduction 65

CJ's Clues

Place value tells you how much numerals are worth. Look at **25**.

```
         tens           ones
25 =   ||||||||||       |||||
       ||||||||||
```

The first numeral tells you how many groups of **tens** there are (2 tens or 20). The second numeral tells you how many **ones** there are (5 ones).

How many fish should we put in our tank? **Count each group of fish under Tens, then count the fish under Ones. Add them together and write the total number of fish on the line.**

Tens　　　　　　　　**Ones**

　　and　　=　_____

　　and　　=　_____

　　and　　=　_____

　　and　　=　_____

66　Place Value

Oh, no! Edison has fallen in. Let's help him. **Read the numerals and words in each fish. What do they equal? Write the answer on the line.**

4 tens and 3 ones = _____

7 tens and 9 ones = _____

8 tens and 1 one = _____

5 tens and 0 ones = _____

3 tens and 6 ones = _____

Can you show the tens and ones for 99?

_____ tens and _____ ones

Great job! Put your stamp sticker on your passport and jump ahead to the next level!

CJ's Clues

When you see three numerals, this means the number is made up of hundreds, tens, and ones. **312** has **3** groups of hundreds, **1** group of tens, and **2** groups of ones.

We've fallen into an underwater world! Let's look for the Lost City. We'll need the secret number to find our way. **Use this shell code to figure out which numerals to write on the lines.**

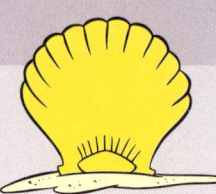 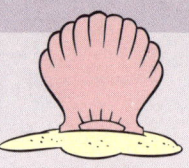 

hundreds   tens   ones

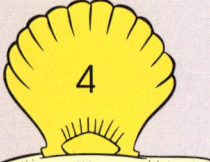 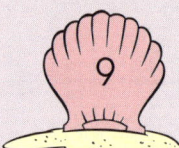  = _____

 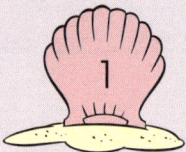  = _____

 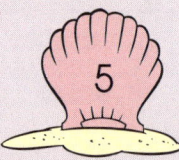  = _____

 =

 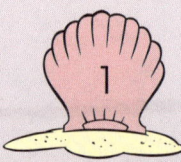  = _____

The secret number is the largest number you wrote. Write it on the line.

_____

Place Value

The secret number got us to the Lost City. Look at all the sea stars! **Can you write the place value for the numerals you see on each?**

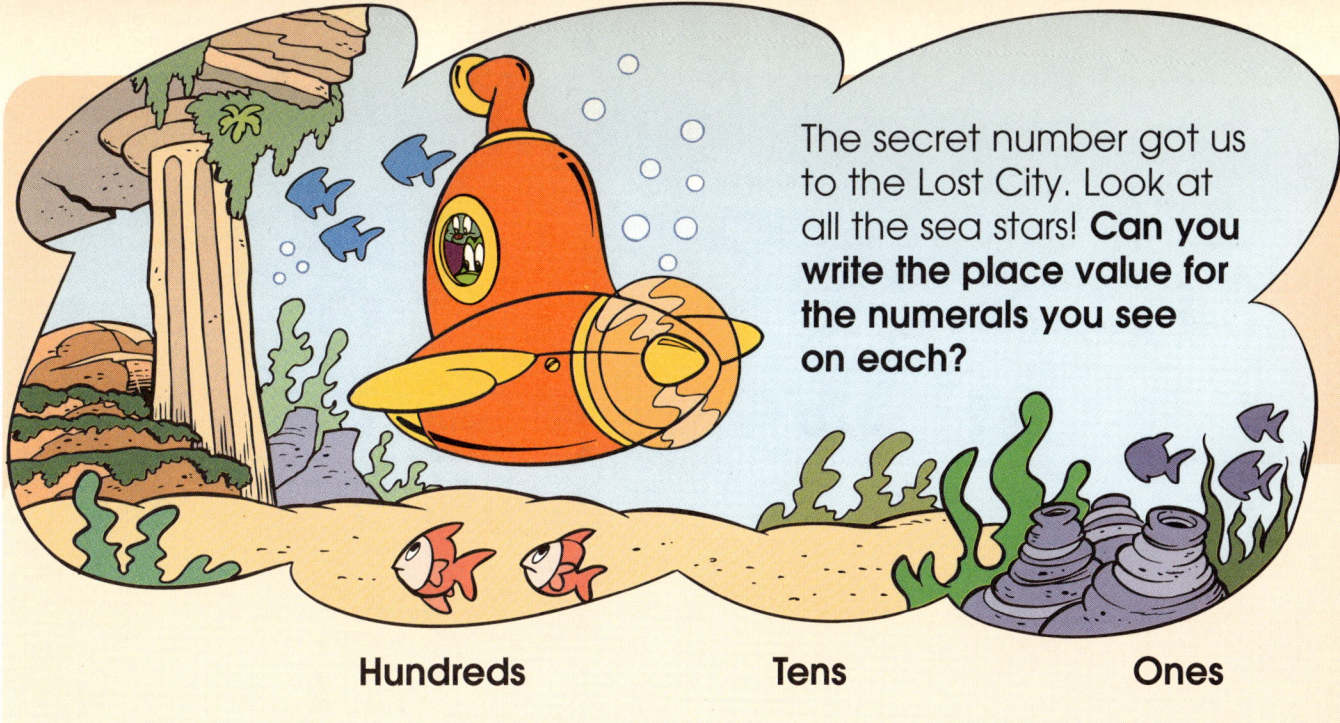

	Hundreds	Tens	Ones
235	______	______	______
401	______	______	______
176	______	______	______
529	______	______	______
340	______	______	______

Can you think of a number in the hundreds that has the same numeral in all three places? Write it on the line. ______

How far down have we gone? **Put these numbers in the right places to show how deep we are. Start with the smallest number.**

| 134 | 8 | 249 | 376 | 25 |

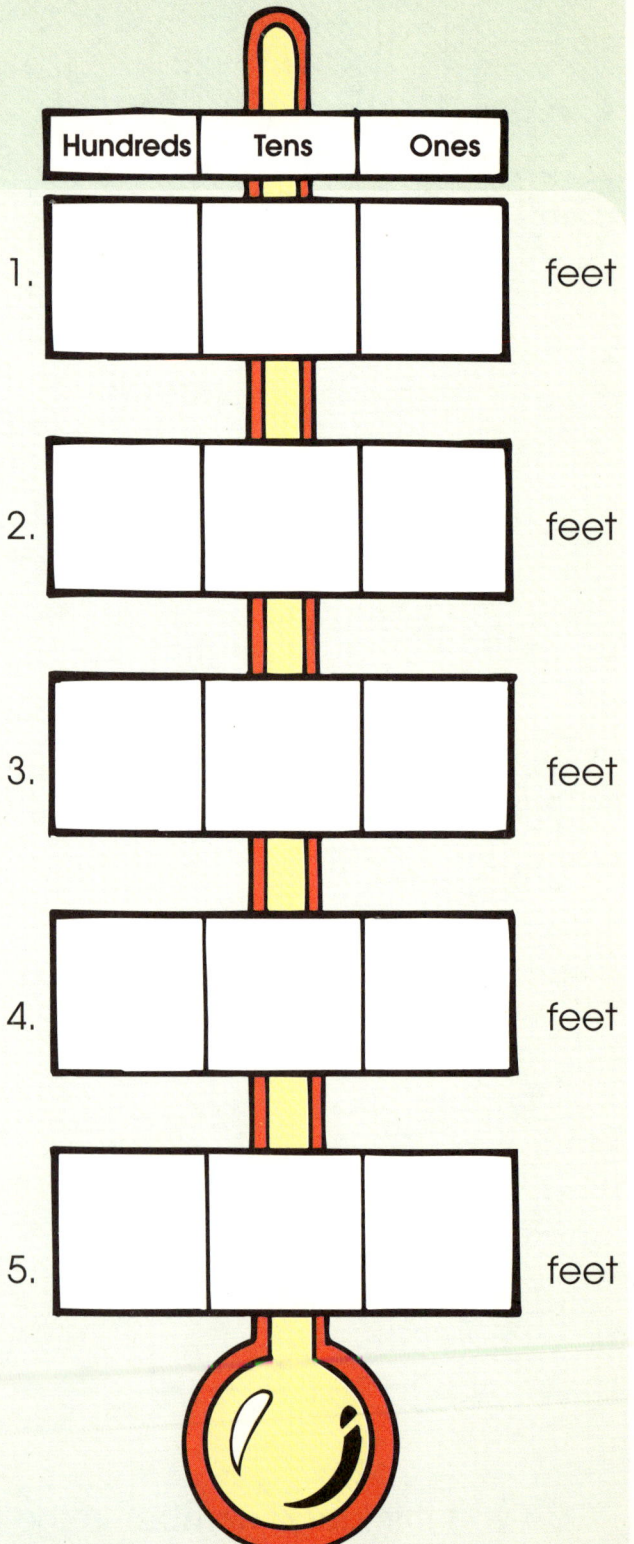

Hundreds | Tens | Ones

1. _____ feet
2. _____ feet
3. _____ feet
4. _____ feet
5. _____ feet

Place Value

Let's find our friend Sir Seahorse. **Help us read the addresses in his underwater neighborhood. Write the numerals in the boxes.**

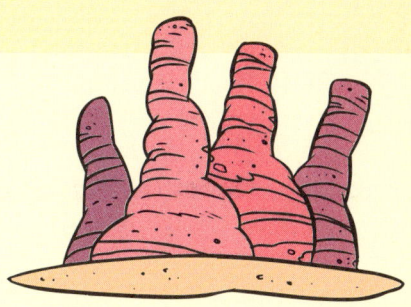

1 hundred + 8 tens + 0 ones

9 hundreds + 6 tens + 2 ones

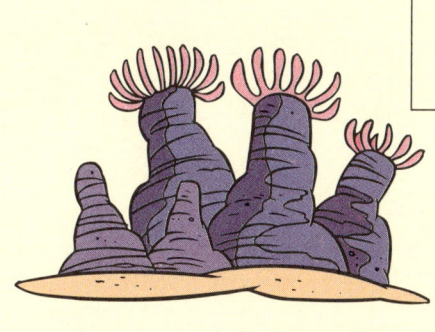

6 hundreds + 4 tens + 7 ones

2 hundreds + 0 tens + 3 ones

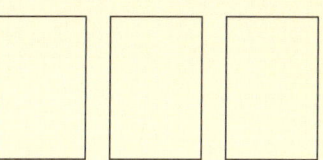

5 hundreds + 9 tens + 1 one

Sir Seahorse lives at 203 Underwater Lane. Circle his house.

You're out of this world! Put your stamp sticker on your passport and jump ahead!

Place Value

CJ's Clues

A number that has 3 numerals is made up of hundreds, tens, and ones, like 203. A number that has 4 numerals is made up of **thousands**, hundreds, tens, and ones, like **4**,572.

Welcome! Come meet my friends. Read each sentence. What number does it describe? **Draw a line to the number to see who's who.**

There are 4 thousands, 3 hundreds, 7 tens, and 6 ones.

There are 6 thousands, 2 hundreds, 1 ten, and 9 ones.

There are 8 thousands, 8 hundreds, 0 tens, and 3 ones.

There are 1 thousand, 2 hundreds, 5 tens, and 4 ones.

Write the numbers from most to least on the lines below.

_____ _____ _____ _____

Some of my pearls are missing! I need to know what's in each chest, so I can see how many are gone. **Look at the value of the pearls and write the numeral on each line to see the total number in each chest.**

= 1,000
= 100
= 10
= 1

_____ , _____ _____ _____

_____ , _____ _____ _____

_____ , _____ _____ _____

_____ , _____ _____ _____

Splendid! Put your stamp sticker on your passport and jump ahead!

Place Value

The Code

A. 9 tens + 6 ones
B. 3 hundreds + 7 tens + 0 ones
C. 5 thousands + 2 hundreds + 1 ten + 4 ones
D. 6 hundreds + 2 tens + 5 ones
E. 8 thousands + 1 hundred + 7 tens + 3 ones
F. 5 tens + 8 ones
G. 7 hundreds + 0 tens + 4 ones
H. 2 thousands + 6 hundreds + 4 tens + 1 one
I. 9 hundreds + 3 tens + 2 ones
J. 1 hundred + 8 tens + 6 ones

You did it! Place your snorkeling gear sticker on the Certificate of Completion and jump ahead.

CJ's Clues

When you add numbers, always start with the **ones column,** on the **right side.** Then add the **tens,** on the **left side.**

Let's look for some of the missing pearls. **Add the ones and tens in each shell. Write the sum below the line.**

```
  1 6        2 4              3 3
+   2      +   1            +   5
-----      -----            -----
  1 8
```

```
  2 1        8 8
+ 5 6      + 1 0
-----      -----
```

```
  7 3       1 2              1 8
+ 2 2      + 1 6            + 2 1
-----      -----            -----
```

Circle the sums in the shells with the pearls. Are these numbers odd or even? _____

(76) Addition •

These sea stars might know where the pearls are. **Solve all these equations, and maybe they'll help us. Write the sums.**

$$10 + 2$$

$$21 + 5$$

$$36 + 1$$

$$50 + 10$$

$$25 + 41$$

$$43 + 11$$

$$22 + 36$$

$$14 + 23$$

$$18 + 30$$

Now circle all the starfish holding pearls. How many pearls are there altogether? _____

CJ's Clues

When you are adding hundreds, first add the **ones** on the **right side**. Then add the **tens** in the **middle**. Then add the **hundreds** on the **left**.

Help! These eels are stealing pearls. **Find all the sums so we can keep track of the pearls.**

```
  113
+ 102
-----
```

```
  524
+ 303
-----
```

```
  780
+ 219
-----
```

```
  234
+ 513
-----
```

```
  321
+ 213
-----
```

```
  463
+ 122
-----
```

```
  506
+ 252
-----
```

```
  230
+ 609
-----
```

```
  111
+ 121
-----
```

```
  260
+ 730
-----
```

```
  129
+ 410
-----
```

```
  144
+ 355
-----
```

Addition

Oh, no! That giant squid is hot on our trail! **Find all the sums to help us escape.**

```
  4 1 8        7 8 2
+ 1 0 1      + 1 0 6
-------      -------

              4 0 5
            + 2 9 4
            -------

  6 0 7        5 7 5
+ 1 2 0      + 2 1 3
-------      -------

  2 5 7        8 3 2
+ 3 4 1      + 1 2 6
-------      -------

  2 6 5        1 4 6
+ 6 3 0      + 4 3 3
-------      -------
```

What's the highest sum? _____

What's the lowest sum? _____

Addition 79

Maybe some pearls are hidden in this school of fish.
Find these sums.

```
  510        200        671
+ 379      + 199      + 208
-----      -----      -----
```

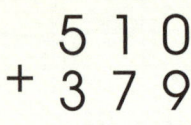

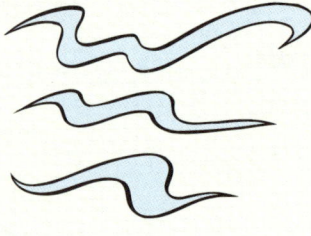

```
  101        356        264
+ 102      + 543      + 201
-----      -----      -----
```

Circle all the sums that are greater than 500.

That looks like Grinsalot, the shark. He's just the kind of fish to take some pearls — or eat a frog! **Add up these equations and help us get out of here!**

```
 111      367      542      177      231
+465     +122     +101     +212     +460
────     ────     ────     ────     ────
```

```
 245          730
+302         +212
────         ────


 845          160
+103         + 12
────         ────
```

Splendid! Put your stamp sticker on your passport and jump ahead to the next level.

Addition

CJ's Clues

Sometimes you have to **regroup** when you add:

```
  ¹49
+   9
-----
   58
```

9 and 9 is 18, and 18 is 1 group of ten and 8 ones. So, write the 8 in the ones column and **carry** the 1 over to the tens column. 1 ten plus 4 tens is 5 tens.

Let's do a little diving! Watch out for the eels! **Find these sums to make them go away. Don't forget to regroup.**

```
  ¹
   39              83              67
 + 45            + 97            +  4
 ----            ----            ----
   84
```

```
   22                            496
 + 79                          + 281
 ----                          -----
```

```
  298                            597
 +604                          + 328
 ----                          -----
```

```
  124
 +589
 ----
```

Now circle the sums less than 100.

We're lost in this seaweed forest. **Help us find our way out by finding the correct sums.**

```
  6 8          1 6          2 3
+ 1 2        + 3 9        + 1 7
-----        -----        -----
```

```
  6 2 4        3 7          8 3 9        4 5
+ 7 9 6      + 2 5        + 1 6 2      + 7 6
-------      -----        -------      -----
```

```
  5 3 2
+ 7 0 9
-------
```

Thanks! Put your stamp sticker on your passport and jump ahead.

Addition 83

We are almost back to Sir Seahorse's house. Help us keep going. **Solve the subtraction equations in our tunnel maze.**

Find the difference that's an odd number greater than 15, but less than 35. That's the tunnel to Sir Seahorse's house. Circle it!

Great job! Put your stamp sticker on your passport and jump ahead to the next level.

Color Code
Red = 24
Blue = 51
Orange = 43
Yellow = 36
Green = 15

We found the pearls and brought them back to Sir Seahorse, so he gave each of us math medals. **Find the differences in the equations on each. Then color our medals according to the code.**

A crab brought us a message. What does it say? **Solve the equations below to find out.**

$$653 - 231$$

$$599 - 472$$

$$324 - 111$$

$$786 - 470$$

$$476 - 123$$

$$946 - 512$$

$$735 - 604$$

Decode the message!
Match the answers and write the letters on the lines.

a = 422
s = 213
t = 127
k = 353
r = 316
h = 434
c = 131

___ ___ ___ ___ ___
213 434 422 316 353

___ ___ ___ ___ ___ ___ !
422 127 127 422 131 353

Watch out for sharks! Let's build a wall to protect us. **Solve the equations so we can use each rock.**

```
  399
- 157
-----
```

```
  134
- 112
-----
```

```
  654
- 502
-----
```

```
  825
- 713
-----
```

```
  572
- 341
-----
```

```
  915
- 804
-----
```

```
  413
- 313
-----
```

```
  851
- 321
-----
```

```
  637
- 516
-----
```

```
  983
- 720
-----
```

We have a brave friend to help us! The sharks are on the run! **Find the differences for these equations to make the sharks go away even faster!**

```
  489         561
- 327       - 321
-----       -----
```

```
  890         777         598
- 490       - 333       - 423
-----       -----       -----
```

```
  309         145
- 108       - 144
-----       -----
```

```
  265
- 254
-----
```

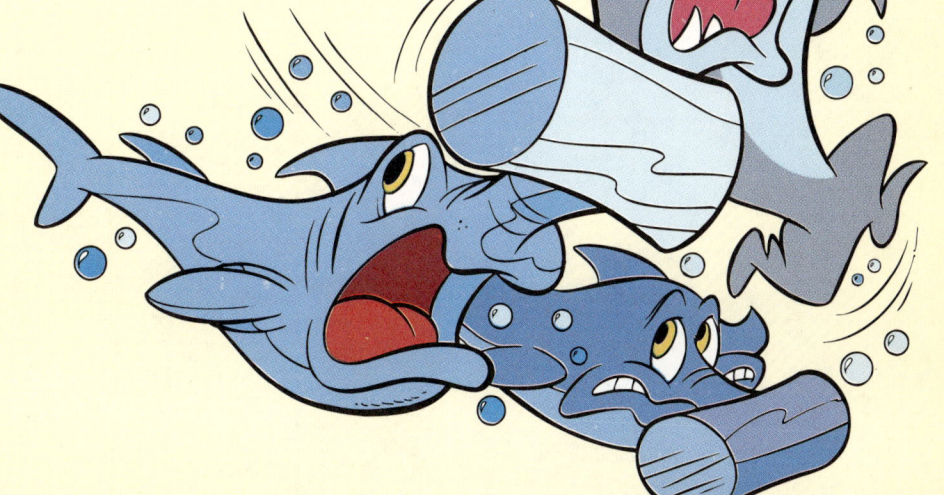

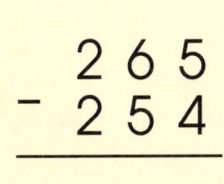

You're the best! Put your stamp sticker on your passport and jump ahead.

CJ's Clues

Sometimes you have to **borrow** to subtract.

$$\begin{array}{r} {}^3\cancel{4}{}^{1}3 \\ -\ 25 \\ \hline 18 \end{array}$$

Here, borrowing one group of 10 will add 10 ones to 3. That gives you 13. Now you'll have one less group of tens in the tens column. You have 13−5 = 8 in the ones and 3−2 =1 in the tens. So the answer is 18.

Now let's have some music! But we're playing the wrong instruments! **Solve all the equations. Then draw a line from the animal to the instrument with the same numerals or differences.**

(frog)	$\begin{array}{r}15\\-\ 8\\\hline 7\end{array}$	$\begin{array}{r}71\\-47\\\hline\end{array}$	(saxophone)
(fly)	$\begin{array}{r}23\\-18\\\hline\end{array}$	$\begin{array}{r}13\\-\ 6\\\hline 7\end{array}$	(drums)
(octopus)	$\begin{array}{r}34\\-26\\\hline\end{array}$	$\begin{array}{r}118\\-\ 89\\\hline\end{array}$	(harp)
(shrimp)	$\begin{array}{r}92\\-68\\\hline\end{array}$	$\begin{array}{r}14\\-\ 9\\\hline\end{array}$	(guitar)
(jellyfish)	$\begin{array}{r}112\\-\ 83\\\hline\end{array}$	$\begin{array}{r}22\\-14\\\hline\end{array}$	(harmonica)

It's time for us to leave the Lost City. All our new friends will see us off! **Help us say a friendly good-bye by helping them subtract these equations.**

$$\begin{array}{r} 28 \\ -19 \\ \hline \end{array}$$

$$\begin{array}{r} 73 \\ -46 \\ \hline \end{array} \quad \begin{array}{r} 521 \\ -489 \\ \hline \end{array} \quad \begin{array}{r} 81 \\ -63 \\ \hline \end{array} \quad \begin{array}{r} 127 \\ -119 \\ \hline \end{array}$$

$$\begin{array}{r} 270 \\ -192 \\ \hline \end{array} \quad \begin{array}{r} 113 \\ -89 \\ \hline \end{array}$$

Great job! Put your stamp sticker on your passport and jump ahead.

We found our way back to the clubhouse! A special sea animal helped us. Would you like to know who? **Play a special game of connect the dots. First, solve all the subtraction equations. Then draw a line to connect the numbers. Start with the answer 1. Find the next highest numeral, then the next highest, and so on. Who do you see?**

```
  5 0 2        8 4 5
- 1 0 1      - 3 1 2

  6 3 9
- 2 4 2

  4 6 7        8 3 6
- 2 1 3      - 5 9 1
```

You're an underwater adventurer! Put your giant clam sticker on your Certificate of Completion!

Review 95

Answer Key

PAGE 66	16, 37, 54, 28
PAGE 67	43, 79, 81, 50, 36; 9 tens, 9 ones
PAGE 68	632, 491, 718, 356, 217; 718
PAGE 69	235, 401, 176, 529, 340; answers will vary
PAGE 70	(grid: 8; 2,5; 1,3,4; 2,4,9; 3,7,6)
PAGE 71	180, 962, 647, ⓐ203, 591
PAGE 72	4,376/stingray 6,219/butterfly fish 8,803/sea turtle 1,254/jellyfish 8,803; 6,219; 4,376; 1,254
PAGE 73	3,315; 1,472; 3,056; 2,168
PAGES 74–75	A. 96 B. 370 C. 5,214 D. 625 E. 8,173 F. 58 G. 704 H. 2,641 I. 932 J. 186
PAGE 76	⑱, 25, ㉘, 77, ㊈, 95, ㉘, 39; even
PAGE 77	⑫, ㉖, 37, ㊿, ㊻, 54, 58, 37, ㊽; 11
PAGE 78	215, 827, 999, 747, 534, 585, 758, 839; 232, 990, 539, 499
PAGE 79	519, 888, 699, 727, 788, 598, 958, 895, 579; 958; 519
PAGE 80	⑧⑧⑨, 399, ⑧⑦⑨, 203, ⑧⑨⑨, 465
PAGE 81	576, 489, 643, 389, 691, 942, 547, 948, 172
PAGE 82	⑧④, 180, ⑦①, 101, 777, 902, 925, 713
PAGE 83	80, 55, 40, 1,420, 62, 1,001, 121, 1,241
PAGES 84–85	56, 68, 48, 894, 124, 877, 643, 94
PAGE 86	73, 12, 30, 51, 83, 17, 11, 13, 58; Grinsalot
PAGE 87	76, ㉑, 32, 12, 24, 52, 50, 3
PAGE 88	24 (red), 43 (orange), 43 (orange), 24 (red), 51 (blue), 15 (green), 36 (yellow), 51 (blue)
PAGE 89	422, 127, 213, 316, 353, 434, 131; Shark attack!
PAGE 90	242, 22, 152, 112, 231, 111, 100, 530, 121, 263
PAGE 91	162, 240, 400, 444, 175, 201, 1, 11
PAGE 92	7—CJ & drums 5—Edison & guitar 8—octopus & harmonica 24—shrimp & tuba 29—jellyfish & harp
PAGE 93	9, 27, 32, 18, 8, 24, 78
PAGES 94–95	1, 2, 3, 11, 32, 76, 133, 136, 167, 245, 254, 397, 401, 533, 614, 629